Aphorisms, Adages & Advice for the Children I Never Had

Wisdom in Time-Tested Sayings from a Man Who Has Been There

LEN TOMAKA

WESTBOW
PRESS®
A DIVISION OF THOMAS NELSON
& ZONDERVAN

WestBow Press books may be ordered through booksellers or by contacting:

WestBow Press
A Division of Thomas Nelson & Zondervan
1663 Liberty Drive
Bloomington, IN 47403
www.westbowpress.com
1 (866) 928-1240

Because of the dynamic nature of the Internet, any web addresses or links contained in this book may have changed since publication and may no longer be valid. The views expressed in this work are solely those of the author and do not necessarily reflect the views of the publisher, and the publisher hereby disclaims any responsibility for them.

Any people depicted in stock imagery provided by Thinkstock are models, and such images are being used for illustrative purposes only. Certain stock imagery © Thinkstock.

ISBN: 978-1-5127-5609-8 (sc)
ISBN: 978-1-5127-5610-4 (hc)
ISBN: 978-1-5127-5608-1 (e)

Library of Congress Control Number: 2016914591

Print information available on the last page.

WestBow Press rev. date: 9/12/2016

Acknowledgments

My gratitude to Terry and Lanny Passaro, Tim Schellhardt, tennis pro Mo Radaoui, Dick Maddrell, Jethro Hurt, Kevin Ladesic D.D.S., and Janet McDonald for their input to get my project to fruition.

Contents

BEHAVIOR

WORK

PEOPLE

TIDBITS

PREFACE
Too Soon Old, Too Late Smart

Over the course of my life, I have happened upon sayings that apply to specific situations in our lives. Actually, they relate powerful lessons. Over time, I jotted many down and placed them in a cigar box. These "real world" insights, to a large degree, have become my wisdoms. As the box became full I began to compile a more formal list of my personal experiences that I expected to pass along to my children.

I was married for thirteen years, then we divorced. We were not blessed with children so I passed these sayings along to apprentices who worked with me, and the lessons were well received. Now I wish to spread them to a larger audience—*to the children and grandchildren I never had.*

To the parents who read this, I acknowledge that my list refers to many situations with which you might already be familiar, but some of them may have slipped through the cracks in your advice to your children.

If I had children or grandchildren, I would share the knowledge in this book with them. And who passed along many of these lessons to me? … my dad, family members, teachers, and many of the tradesmen with whom I have had the pleasure of working. Who can benefit from reading these lessons? Anyone of any age actually can draw from these lessons—whether one is working, playing, or just attending the school of hard knocks.

BEHAVIOR

B1 Sidestepping a Committee

It is better to reject a committee assignment than to commit and not do much at all. If you have a busy schedule, accept that you can't deliver what is expected of committee members. Everyone will understand because we're all busy. Instead, consider suggesting that you serve as a consultant or as someone to bounce an occasional idea off of.

B2 If Something Seems Too Good
To Be True, It Usually Is

When someone proposes a deal that sounds simply too good to be true, be wary. Do as much research as you can. Ask many questions about unforeseen problems that might arise to help determine your opinion of the offer.

B3 Whoever Breaks the Silence Loses

In many sales or negotiation meetings, the professionals employ a trick: silence. If most of the facts are on the table from both sides and a lull emerges in the conversation, the first to speak normally is considered to be more anxious to complete the deal or to be in the weaker position. So take action by being quiet.

B4 Betrayal

Along life's journey, you are apt to be betrayed. The closer you are to the people who betray you, the deeper the hurt. Realize there's another side to the story and you should listen to the circumstances on the other side. For example, I was going to buy an item from a friend for fifty dollars. But when I saw him a few days later, he said, "Oh, I don't have that item for you anymore because Bobby offered me ninety dollars and I sold it to him." I was livid because he had broken his word. I had figured the deal was done, but it wasn't. From his point of view he got a better offer, it was merely business and I would have done the same thing. NO, I wouldn't have. I would have honored the original deal. The lesson: *Put it in writing*. As you get older, you will face similar deals. *Put it in writing*. If something goes wrong, you'll have the agreement in front of you. Also recognize that betrayal in personal matters can prove even more devastating.

B5 Don't Anticipate a Bad Experience

It only stretches out the bad experience. Take, for example, a dental appointment. You can't control what happens there, but you can make yourself crazy anticipating it. Try to say "I can't wait to get to this dentist appointment tomorrow and get it behind me." (Besides, if it's only teeth cleaning, your teeth will look and feel so good afterward.)

B6   A Little Knowledge Is a Dangerous Thing

The phrase originated in An Essay on Criticism by Alexander Pope. If you have limited knowledge about a certain matter, don't try to come off as an authority on the subject to those listening. If other people know more than you, they will recognize you are bluffing. If they take it further and expose you, you will look like a real jerk. Be careful.

B7 | I Need, *Not* I Want

The words "I need" highlight the giver (or enabler) to the person who is listening. Conversely, the words "I want" tend to make that person defensive. Keep that in mind when you approach someone for help or to accommodate you.

B8 Hearing Is Not Listening

There's a big difference between listening to somebody and just hearing that person. That's why when you watch a TV newscast and a reporter interviews somebody at the scene of an accident, that reporter nods his or her head. This indicates that - "I'm listening to you and absorbing what you have to say and want you to say more." But nodding can't be automatic. Make sure you are absorbing and thinking about what the other person is saying. Ask follow-up questions. This is what makes for true communication.

If you noticing that the person to whom you are talking is not focused on what you are saying you can say, "You're hearing me but you're not listening to me."

B9 Creative Visualization

This is a powerful tool, especially as you prepare for a professional or social meeting, because you can go over several items beforehand in your mind and anticipate responses. If someone says this, you can respond with that. You will be better prepared and won't have to think on the fly.

B10 A Shot Across the Bow

A naval expression, it means an armed vessel has fired a shot in front of another vessel as a final warning of an intention to aim its next shot to strike the vessel. This is a good expression to use with your peers when you want to get across that you mean business in a negotiation. "Let's throw a shot across their bow."

B11 Addressing Racism

As long as we inhabit separate little worlds and build separate little fortresses from some cultural or ethnic or monetary point of view, we will never be one as a people. While the situation is slowly, but surely, getting better, problems and divisions will persist. Up to age eleven, this inner-city kid went to a charity summer camp where ethnic groups of kids were thrown in together. I learned in camp that a bully was a bully, wheelers/dealers were wheelers /dealers, and lazy kids were just that. I took each kid on his or her own terms. I preferred judging my peers not by the color of their skin but by their actions. I was quite comfortable with that, but while attending a seminar later on race issues, I was taught that, in fact, if I am white and am working with a black person, we should acknowledge that, "Hey, I'm white and you're black. That's a fact. So what?" We should realize we come from different places and we are here in unity. I learned that's a better approach. As our world shrinks because of our ever-expanding technology, we all grow closer together.

B12 Less Is More

Originated by poet Robert Browning, this phrase was made famous as characterizing the minimalist design style of architect Ludwig Mies van der Rohe. This is also about being classy. If you have a person over the barrel in a situation, just cool it and show some class. Don't go for the jugular vein. You will emerge showing a lot of style that will be remembered, as will all the lessons here.

B13 Aggression

When I was a lay ministry team member at a church, the training involved learning about aggressive, assertive, and passive behavior. This proved extremely important. When I was younger and someone became aggressive with me, I would match that aggression, bringing myself to his level. As I became older and wiser, I learned to take a deep breath and absorb what other people were saying, not how they were saying it. Hopefully, that would temper the aggressive person's attitude. The point is to address the facts. You also will learn there is a time to be aggressive, a time to be assertive, and a time to be passive – and there's a response for each. A good rule of thumb is that when you must work things out, go over the facts and show why you came to your conclusion and, thus, your action. Seek to leave emotions out of it.

B14 A Reputation Takes Every Minute to Build

Do not lose your reputation with one indiscretion. That one imprudent act, social or professional, can erase all that you've worked to obtain.

B15 Living Well Is the Best Revenge

If you've been wronged and it's still possible to go on as if it didn't matter, do it. That attitude trumps the carrying of grudges or worrying about getting even. It often pays to avoid hatred and other negative thoughts and, instead, focus on standing tall, and getting on with your life. You can control doing that.

B16   Fight Fire with Fire

Aside from being a song by Metallica, this saying refers to the time when all conversation and arbitration fails and there is no way to avoid a confrontation. Fight back in the same manner in which you're attacked. When a salesperson knocks on your door to sell you a book on religion try to get the salesperson to buy one of your books on religion.

B17 Past, Present, and Future

Live in the now and plan for the future. Don't dwell on the past and certainly don't live in it. Don't hold onto a memory or a dream that takes time away from being productive. You may be holding yourself back from going forward. Yes, if you're just getting over a relationship, a divorce, or a death, there is a time to grieve, a time for anger, and a time to recuperate. And every one of us differs in the time it takes to work out from underneath a calamity. But sulking or pouting isn't positive; it simply deters you from starting anew.

B18   If It Is to Be, It Is Up to Me

This was a book published by Thomas B. Smith, Michael A Markowski, and Marjorie L Markowski. If you want to make something happen, be an integral part of making it happen. If you can't do it alone and you have teammates to help you, make sure they are active. Don't sit on your hands waiting for them to do their part. That's especially true if you're a "foundation" type of person who requires a "skyscraper" type of colleague to complete the structure. That skyscraper persona is usually a Type A personality and a foundation person usually isn't. The skyscraper will often do what he or she desires; and if that happens, be sure it's in your best interest.

B19 The Best That You Can Be

I've gone from working with the tools on jobsites to various corporate posts in my industry, but I've always held my union card. That's because between corporate roles I would take a job as a pipefitter. It is quite a different hat, but it's always okay to say, "I'm going to be the best pipefitter I can be" rather than, "Oh, I really need to get back into the comfortable office." Focus on being the best you can be at whatever you are doing. Regret is a by-product of not giving your best effort.

B20 Don't Judge Another Man Until You've Walked in His Moccasins

This is a lesson in perspective. The jury system is supposed to be a peer group that knows the pluses and minuses of your lifestyle, especially when dealing with people from other cultures. When dealing with those whose culture is unfamiliar, don't be quick to judge them until you understand how their life experiences differ from yours.

B21 What's Important at This Time?

What's important to you today won't be as important down the road because you'll be a different you. Just think of the years behind you and what your brain has absorbed since you were ten, then perhaps fifteen, then twenty and so on. Having experienced those milestones and many others, I certainly was a different person with different attitudes and habits at each of those points in time. Situations I stressed over then do not faze me now because I have the confidence to handle them.

B22 Lend Money - Not So Fast

Don't lend anyone money is a wonderful rule. Yet, if certain people tug at your heart strings you are considering lending them money, get something of equal or greater value to hold in return. And get a written agreement signed by both of you that makes clear that, after a certain amount of time, if the money hasn't been paid back in full, you acquire possession of that item. Take it from me, because I was burned time and again years ago. Nobody teaches this lesson in school.

B23 Don't Ever Cosign on Someone Else's Loan

You have nothing to gain and everything to lose by cosigning on someone's loan. Those who ask you to do so are in dire straits; they weren't approved on their own equity or merits, so they ask you to bail them out with your good name to get their loan. There's a reason that they're not in good shape. If they drop the ball on this loan, you are responsible and you will have to make the situation right with the lender. Love them to pieces, but don't cosign on any loans for them.

B24 Avoid Procrastination

Procrastination is the opposite of action. So try the "Swiss cheese" method of getting things done. Think of the entire task as a piece of cheese and then nibble off parts of it. By making holes in that workload, in time you will consume the entire cheese. The task is complete.

B25 Love/Hate Relationships

If you find yourself in one, good luck. The battles and arguments of such a relationship are horrible. Try to have a relationship that evens out, one that is healthy and solid. Naturally, rough roads are part of the game and part of maturing, but when they are rough all the time, reconsider that relationship.

B26 Crisis after Crisis: That's Life

Get used to it. As you grow older, obstacles may emerge in every direction you take, no matter what. Don't fall into the "Why me?" attitude. That's life. Do your best at working through one crisis after another. (I wish you the best of luck.)

B27 To Grow, You Must Leave Something Behind

A snake sheds its skin and slithers away for another adventure. Human beings also progress and grow, either professionally or socially, when we leave one place to get to the next. In the process, we use what we've learned so we can grow further. It is very difficult if you want to move forward and your partner wants to stay in one place. Recognize you will have to change and leave some negative ideas behind if your goals are set for a higher level. Change is very difficult for all of us. So think of it as 'modification with no limitations.'

B28 It's Always Darkest before the Dawn / There's Light at the End of the Tunnel

If you are in a situation that is bleak and getting bleaker, this is a good reminder to persist as long as you're on a solid path and still believe the situation will turn around. Stay the course, stick with it, and get it done.

B29 Gut Feeling

Having a hunch means that past experiences are coming back to you and trying to tell you something. Or, perhaps, you have seen other people contend with a certain experience. You can't really pinpoint it, but you're quite sure which way the situation will turn out. *Always* respect your gut feeling, especially if it's telling you to wait before making a decision. This is very powerful stuff.

B30 Take the Bitter with the Sweet

Every situation or project you will engage in will include negative surprises along the way. This advice reminds us to "roll with the punches" and do not be discouraged by temporary setbacks.

B31 Automatic Alarm

If you meet somebody new and either something bothers you about the person or you're attracted to that person, your automatic alarms try to pick up that person's aura and energy. Will the new acquaintance mesh with yours or will a conflict develop? This is your automatic alarm. As you age, certain situations will occur and spark instances of deja vu. Be aware that these situations are universal. We all get them. Try to acknowledge it. Paying attention of that alarm will benefit personal and business relationships.

B32 Don't Bluff a Bluffer

This is a natural response to someone who is trying to put something over on you and you see through it, so you push back with the same behavior. There's a bit of transference occurring here because you're showing that you're just like the other person and aware of all the tricks. Another way to say it is, "Don't steal from a thief."

B33 Keep TV and the Internet in Check

If you want to veg out and relax a bit, that's perfectly okay. But realize your life stops during the time that you do it. If you watch television because you have nothing else to do, that's not good. If you're ill and resting and watching whatever is on, that's different and acceptable. You will gain so much more by reading, or listening to an educational recording, or taking a walk. Watching a sitcom doesn't make sense to me. The same holds true with Internet games. Control the time you spend on them and beware of becoming mesmerized by them.

B34 It's a Gray Area

In any disagreement, you must always recognize the other person possesses a different point of view. Try, as would an arbitrator, to see the gray areas where you both overlap and agree. Once you settle on the agreed-upon items, try to expand on the rest of the items involved.

B35 Never Look a Gift Horse in the Mouth

First attributed to St. Jerome in the 4th century regarding looking at a horses' teeth to tell the age of a horse that was a donation (a gift horse). But by today's standards, accept any gift for what it is, a gift. Keep any disappointment to yourself. It's quite like a year-end bonus. Don't make any assumptions about the level of generosity that will go into that decision. You've no place to go but downhill if you fret or complain about its size. It's all extra anyway. And don't take it personally. Accept it graciously.

B36 Why Worry?

We all worry, but worrying solves nothing. It is a waste of time. Rather than worry, simply focus on whether you did all you could. Ask yourself, "Is there any stone left unturned in this matter?"

B37 Get a World Atlas or Globe

Even with the Internet at our fingertips, reviewing an atlas every now and then helps you to grasp how vast our world is compared to the little corner we inhabit. It also gives you a perspective on how many different cultures and nationalities the world is composed of. Knowing your geography helps you ground yourself in the world.

B38 Travelling: It Will Make You Well-Rounded

You can learn lots of lessons from other cultures while traveling, especially as our world gets smaller. Travel creates lifetime memories. Not only does the experience enrich you, by recalling them with someone who also has visited the same region can make a very enjoyable conversation.

B39 Face the Dragon

As children, many of us were told bedtime stories involving a beautiful princess, a deadly, powerful dragon, and a handsome young prince with a sword riding a white charger. Those images are the images of life. The beautiful princess is the prize one seeks. The dragon is the obstacle. The sword is the instrument for slaying the dragon. The prince must find the dragon's soft spot and thrust the sword there to defeat the dragon so both prince and princess can live happily ever after. The tale's moral is that the dragon is the obstacle, and the princess is the goal. If you are the prince, you must act accordingly, and use the sword and your skills wisely.

B40 Change of Strategy

Let's talk about boxing. Suppose you're at a ten-round match and one fighter is head and shoulders above the other fighter on points, and he's won nine rounds on points and it's now the last round. The only way the other boxer can win is to knock out his rival. To pull that off, the losing boxer must change his style and go for the knockout. On the other hand, the boxer ahead on points must be prepared for that. You can relate this to any other styles or any other sports in competition.

B41 Loneliness

If you're lonely, look outside. Explore the many things to do right in your neighborhood or city that don't cost too much and will enable you to mingle with people. Take in a museum, stop at a restaurant or a different coffee shop, or circulate at coffee hour after church service or at a farmer's market or outdoor concert. Do not become a sad recluse. My apartment is my solitude where I can relax. I have my music, books, computer, and television there. It is peaceful but I do not want my apartment to turn into a safe jail cell.

B42 Know What *Not* to Do

Knowing what not to do often proves more important than knowing what to do. This is especially true when you are exposed to different cultures. For example, in the United States, if you enjoy a theater performance, it's appropriate to whistle as you applaud. However, in Europe and elsewhere, whistling sends the opposite message. There, you're considered to be booing. Studying a culture before you visit and then observing those around you will help you fit in.

B43 Don't Do the Crime If You Can't Do the Time

This is a hip expression from the 50s. It is a good reminder if you're mulling over the idea of breaking the rules. Answer these questions: What are the consequences? Can I handle them if things don't work out like I want them to?

B44 Cream Rises to the Top

Even if you are living what you consider to be a humdrum existence, do your best at what you're assigned to do and you will be recognized. Don't just blend in with the crowd; be a catalyst.

B45 That's Not Done in This Day and Age

Times change! When I was a youngster, if you grew your hair long or had long sideburns, sported tattoos, lifted weights or rode a motorcycle, either you were Fonzie on the Happy Days television show or you were a hoodlum. Today, long hair is even longer, tattoos have never been more popular, and working out is the thing to do. With youth, it's more about rebellion. When we adopted rock and roll, it was to be different, for the most part, and to gain our own identities with our dances. Each generation adopts its various dance forms. So don't be critical (or, at least, too critical) of young people who seek their own identities. They're different; that doesn't mean they're bad.

B46 Things Take Time

Regarding my first patent, I couldn't believe how many steps were involved and how long the process took. While I was ready and eager for every step, I had to wait for approval and then move to the next clearance until every part of the bureaucracy chain had given their okay. It was like that in construction, too. The response would always be, "We will let you know." The point: Be patient with whatever situation you find yourself in. Patience, you'll learn, helps the time go by.

B47 Roll with the Punches

In boxing, when a fighter takes a punch square on the jaw, it causes more damage than if he has a chance to 'roll his head' as the punch lands. So if bad news strikes you, try to turn it into glancing blows instead of considering it devastating. Think, "I can deal with this." Treat a tragedy or disaster as an annoyance.

B48 Immediate Decisions

In many situations, you likely will reach an initial opinion. But you also may change your mind after, say, a day or two. Don't be forced into making an immediate decision if you don't need to. Absorb information as long as you can until you are comfortable. You might think of it from a different point of view and draw a different conclusion. Or you might reaffirm your initial view. There is something to be said for "Let me sleep on it." I believe that overnight rest gives your subconscious a chance to relax and think things through more clearly.

B49 Never Be the First to Believe, Never Be the Last to Deceive

This is a lyric from the musical *Chess*. Do not be the first to jump in with both feet on a new idea or a fresh sales promotion or a new franchise. Let it develop a little history before you make that full commitment. Conversely, don't be the last person to jack somebody around who's been jacked around eighteen times before. That person might explode and you will be in their crosshairs. You will receive all the punishment instead of those who preceded you.

B50   Be the One Talked About

As gossip runs wild, nobody knows the whole story. Yet, people gossip, saying that you did this or you did that. Don't worry about it. Be the active one even if people talk about you rather than being inactive and gossiping about others.

B51 Retain a Friend

If you go on a blind date or meet someone who makes it known they like you but it's not mutual, don't ever cut off the relationship. Don't be rude with a comment such as, "Listen, this just isn't going to work. I'm out of here." Instead, be gentler and say, "It appears we're not on the same wavelength." You can retain the friendship and use it as a networking tool. You don't know that person's contacts; he or she might have a friend to whom you would be attracted.

B52   First Impressions

Always try to present yourself in the best light when meeting someone for the first time. You never know when that new contact might help you from a networking standpoint. Plus, presenting yourself in your most positive and engaging shows respect for the other person.

B53 You Can Only Help Someone Until You Hurt Yourself

When you're assisting a friend, a relative, or someone in need or hurting, and that person stops taking your advice or rejects your help, recognize that your efforts aren't effective any longer. When you realize this and still try to change that person's ways all you are doing is upsetting yourself. Sure it hurts; but just back off. Let time take its course.

B54 The Battle between Two Wolves

A wonderful American Indian story pertains to daily life. One evening, an old Nez Perce Indian told his grandson about a battle that goes on inside people. "My son, the battle is between two wolves inside us all. One is evil. It is anger, envy, jealousy, sorrow, regret, greed, arrogance, self-pity, resentment, inferiority, lies, false pride, superiority and ego. The other is good. It is joy, peace, love, hope, serenity, humility, kindness, benevolence, empathy, generosity, truth, compassion, and faith." The grandson thought for a minute and then asked his grandfather, "Which one wins?" The old man simply replied, "The one you feed."

B55   When You Assume Something

On the *Odd Couple* TV show, when Oscar didn't do something Felix asked him to do, Oscar explained, "I assumed you would have changed your mind when you found out the price of it!" Felix shouted "Assumed! – You assumed!" Felix then went to the blackboard they kept in their apartment and, in giant letters, wrote ASSUME with chalk and then inserted slash marks to make it read ASS/U/ME. "When you assume something, you just make an *ass* out of *you* and *me*," he asserted. That often proves true in life.

B56 You Can Only Teach What You Know

From a book by motivational speaker Leo Buscaglia comes this thought: "If you only know anger and jealousy, that is all you can teach those around you." The same concept applies to the opposite – love and kindness. Which will you teach?

B57 One Bird in the Hand Is Worth Two in the Bush

This isn't always true. If a situation arises when getting the two birds in the bush is worth the risk of losing the bird in the hand, go for it. But be very careful of losing the bird in the hand; that could trigger a total loss.

B58 Your Environment

Look around. Is your environment conducive to whom you are? Your environs are extremely important to your behavior and your viewpoints. Could the places you go and the things you do be holding you back from growing?

B59 Forgive and Forget

If you forgive someone for hurting you, you don't necessarily need that person's apology.

Forgiveness releases *you* to go forward without holding any "baggage" in your thoughts.

B60   When the Going Gets Tough the Tough Get Going

When you are in a tough spot and things are not going well in any situation, remind yourself of this saying because it will encourage you to hang in there.

B61 Best Relationship Comment

A couple of friends I know were showing me their new car when one of them jokingly snarled "I don't like this color but I AM IN A RELATIONSHIP! But seriously, my partner LIKED this color more than I DID NOT LIKE this color so it's okay with me." What a great way to help finalize different options of going forward.

B62 Oh What a Tangled Web We Weave When First We Practice to Deceive

A Sir Walter Scott (not William Shakespeare) quote, this is very good saying when someone is sharing a plot that they are thinking of which involves telling falsehoods or half-truths. So many times I have seen these situations backfire on them because of their error in assuming that all of the pieces would fall into place and all was lost. Be careful you don't build a house of cards, because if you pull one card from the bottom, the edifice you have built may collapse.

B63 I Have Got You Over a Barrel

This sayings originally described the act of trying to save a drowning victim's life by laying the victim stomach down on top of a barrel laying on its side and rolling the barrel thereby putting pressure on the victims lungs to hopefully extract the water in the lungs. I don't know how well that worked but the phase stayed with us because the rescuer had complete control over the victim. So in today's world, if you have complete control of a situation, you have the other person over a barrel to do your bidding.

B64   Going Straight for the Jugular

In the animal world lions attack their prey by clamping down with their powerful jaws on the throats of the victim, crushing the wind pipe and also stopping the flow of blood to the heart. The lion just holds on tight until the prey is dead. In our world of conflict this is a harsh phase used for an action to end a conflict.

B65 Peeling Away Layers of an Onion

This metaphor refers to people's motives. If people look back upon their motives and 'peel away' layer after layer of emotion, they may discover their own flaws while coming to a conclusion and perhaps change their minds. It is a powerful personal tool and more fair to the people around them.

B66 You Can't See the Forest for the Trees

Linda Ronstadt's song "Different Drum," about the breaking up of a relationship, contains this lyric, which explains how her boy friend just doesn't see the big picture. She doesn't want to be with him anymore. In our lives, it means don't get hung up on all the details and lose sight of the goal.

B67 Don't Put All Your Eggs in One Basket

Don't invest all of your money in one endeavor. It is pretty easy to understand that if you drop the basket, you lose all of your eggs.

B68   You Are Spinning Your Wheels

The basic idea relates to friction. When a hot rod car is competing in a drag race, at the very start the driver puts the gas pedal to the floor to put as much fuel that they possibly can into the engine.

During the initial surge of power, when the engine reacts to the transmission, the transmission spins the tires so fast that the rubber tires lose contact with the road and the tires spin until the friction with the road is regained. The term is 'burning rubber.' The point is that when you see someone putting effort into something with little or no results you can mention this statement to that person.

B69 It's Just Not My Cup of Tea

When someone is impressed with something and they feel you should be impressed also. But you are not impressed. This is a wonderful saying because it doesn't insult the person. You are explaining that you don't agree without demeaning them.

WORK

WI TTLL

Talk to teach, and listen to learn. A veteran salesman explained to me that in any meeting you are there to talk or to listen. If you called the meeting to learn something, you are there to listen. If you called the meeting to share information, you are there to talk. So know the purpose of the meeting and act accordingly.

W2   Squeaky Wheels Get the Grease

In machine shops, when a machine is running rough and needs lubrication, it gets greased. This adage applies to people too. If something is bothering you, speak up and communicate your thoughts. But be careful not to take this out of context. You don't want to become a squeaky person all the time; you could be judged a complainer.

W3 Strike While the Iron Is Hot

This saying comes from blacksmithing. The hot iron is malleable and can be shaped when hot, but once it cools, the shape is permanent. In competitions in which the advantage changes over time (since both sides haven't employed all their tactics or strategies), recognize where the power lies at any particular moment. If it is with you, *act* to close it out. If it is with your opponent, *act* to prolong the action until the tide turns. An iron that's not hot is a lot less proficient than one that is. Take advantage of opportunity.

W4 If It Ain't Broke Don't Fix It

Many procedures (or equipment for that matter) that still work properly needn't be changed just for the sake of change. Do not make a change unless you gain worthwhile benefits. A lot has to do with the costs involved.

W5 Differences Exist among Types of Education

As you meet more people along life's journey, a language barrier will emerge at times. If you are a working-class person, be careful with your slang verbiage and, yes, try to be a bit more refined. If you have a post-graduate degree, remember that a working-class person is just differently educated, not ignorant. I must add that the working-class person probably has lived through more of life's situations than the post-grad who spent a lot more time in study halls. If snobbery exists on the formally educated side, it is balanced by reverse snobbery on the working-class side.

W6 Persistence Pays

With a personal project or if in sales, when given a "no" for the umpteenth time, try again, and again, and again. Sooner or later, someone you approach will like your proposition. . Let it be under your control to determine when you have done all you could do. Be persistent.

W7 The Tail Wags the Dog

Think of organizational structure. When a subordinate decides the direction an entire unit will take, a breakdown of the structure has occurred. It contradicts the established structure and lack of leadership from the top, most always causing friction among those involved.

W8 Keep a Log

A log or diary gives you a chronological reminder of the order of each event in case a problem arises. It clarifies your thinking and illuminates how you arrived at your views. In law, a log cannot be submitted as evidence but it gains you credibility for an organized approach.

W9 Get It Done

Many people who aren't the sharpest are still able to get the job done while others get hung up by debating what should be done. This in itself is an important skill. Someone will notice if you are able to get the job done and do not get caught up in the dull background noise. Get the job done ... and well!

W10   Fix the Right Leak

You know your roof is leaking when you see water stains appear on your ceiling or water running down the wall. It's critical to fix the source of the leak before you fix the wall. But give yourself some time to make sure the leak is, indeed, fixed before repairing and repainting the wall. Look at the problems of life in that light. Are you addressing the real problem and not a superficial condition? Learn to recognize the actual problem and don't get sidetracked by its effects.

WII Time Is *or* Isn't on Your Side

In any situation, whether you face a deadline or not to accomplish something is important. If you can pressure the other side because time is on your side, do it! On the other hand, don't let the other side pressure you to make a decision if you need more time to ponder it.

W12 Don't Sweat the Small Stuff

In 1988 Michael Mantell PhD published this book and also author Richard Carlson published similar books. This is what a friend says when noticing you are overreacting to some minor annoyance as you strive to reach a goal. If you sweat the small stuff you may be identified as a highly intense person. Remember: A distinction exists between being meticulous and being paranoid.

W13 What Have You Done for Me Lately?

This question goes beyond Janet Jackson's song. Be constantly moving forward and active. Don't rest on your laurels, especially in today's corporate world where executive memories are short. Don't fall into the "I've been with this company for fifteen years and a regular cog in the wheel that makes things operate smoothly." Management prefers positive and active people, not just those who find their little groove and stagnate. That probably worked years ago when colleagues said, "Oh boy, Harry has put in thirty years and he's a stalwart." Nowadays, Harry had better handle his load – or else he is at risk of being let go. The past is the past – that's what we all leave behind.

W14   Changing Jobs

If you are eager to switch jobs, get that new position before you quit your current job. And don't bum rap any of your previous colleagues. Negative comments can come back to haunt you.

W15 Job Search

Many times, you won't be given the courtesy of a callback from prospective employers. Don't think it's your fault. Just keep on plugging ahead. Although you certainly can contact that employer with a follow-up, give them a little credit; they often don't have the time to call back all the people who didn't get the job. They deal with those still under consideration for the job. I lived this, and it's devastating when you don't hear back. That's the time to "pick yourself up, dust yourself off and try all over again." Consider that a job search is a process - a job, in itself. Keep moving forward!

W16   If You're Fired

If you're terminated for whatever reason, the shock can be devastating, especially if you are caught by surprise. Keep a positive attitude to your colleagues as long as you're on the job. It doesn't pay to complain or tell off people. It's very risky because it shows lack of character. If your future employer gets wind that you were very disgruntled, especially if they hear that from your previous employer, it won't benefit you. Hold to the view that "when one door closes, another opens."

W17   Focus, Focus, Focus

You hear it a lot, but it's great advice. Concentrate on whatever you're doing. In sports and on the job, it's critical to focus. You don't want to dwell on your mortgage, or that you must paint the fence tomorrow while you are replacing a leaking faucet today. One step at a time is the focus. Concentrate on the task at hand – and nothing else.

W18   Make Eye Contact

While ushering at church, I stood at the front and tried to draw the people forward because it helps to compress churchgoers into a more compact group. If I made eye contact with them, like a magnet, I could get them to walk farther forward. Otherwise, if I didn't make that eye contact, most people would sit farthest away from the front as a sign of humility, I guess. Also, to me, when you look people in the eye, it shows them that, yes, they have your full attention. Eye contact shows sincerity and honesty. Use it in all of your dealings.

W19 Work to Live, Don't Live to Work

Like it or not, in our possession-laden world, you need money to do most everything. If you're working for a paycheck and it's taking so much out of you that, for the most part, you just go home and crash, then that's not a very fulfilling life. However, if your work gives you the ability to enjoy whatever you like to do, that's wonderful! People fortunate enough to stick with the job they enjoy, whether in the arts or elsewhere, rarely have a bad day. And even if a difficult day emerges, they still are in the field that they love.

W20   What Goes Around Comes Around

If you do good deeds for people, it is easier for people to do good deeds for you. Conversely, if you do bad deeds to people, it's easier for people to do bad deeds to you later. Payback on bad deeds always seems to be much worse than the original deed. The Austrians have a saying, "When you sing into the forest, a song will come back to you." Spread good karma. I noticed when I was a young man that the mean cats and dogs in my neighborhood were owned by mean people. It was as if they adopted their owners' personalities, to some degree.

W21 I Don't Remember

In a discussion with those who claim you agreed with them before on an issue that now has become a disagreement, simply employ this response; tell the person, "I do not remember that. I am not saying you're wrong. I just don't remember that." You aren't denying anything, and it gives you time to work on an answer.

W22 Having an Ace in the Hole

This is a gambling term in poker. In five-card stud when four cards are turned up and the other is facedown, the down card is the most important because the other players don't know what it is. So, in any negotiation, show what you have to show, but hold your most powerful strength for last.

W23 What Do You Bring to the Table?

That's a very good question to ask yourself mentally as you look at the people around the table including yourself. It will help you focus as you address the topic at hand by making sure others around you are providing information that explains why they're there. It also will help you identify those who are bluffing their way through the meeting.

W24   You've Got to Swing the Bat to Get a Hit

If you simply stand around watching a situation and don't get active in it, the world will pass you by. You must be involved to reap the benefits. Relate it to a baseball player: By taking the third strike instead of swinging at the ball, he is passing up the chance to get a hit and has nothing to lose if he misses because the pitch is probably a strike anyway.

W25 Keep Busy at Work and at Play

You will find that when you're occupied, your mind will not wander. Personally, I'm much more comfortable being busy. I maintain much more control of a solid personal foundation by being focused.

W26   Find a Mentor

Try to enlist an older or more experienced acquaintance you respect as a mentor. So that you will be able now and then to bounce things off him or her. Explain your interests and abilities so that your mentor will understand how best to advise you and may anticipate how you will react to a given situation. We all could use a little coaching in life.

W27 Don't Win the Battle and Lose the War

Keep your eye on the big picture. If there are levels to be completed along the way to the finish, stay alert and don't relax along the way. You just may go into a zone of complacency, and it may be too early to relax your efforts.

W28   Knowledge Is Power

Think about it. The sports figure, the executive, the tradesman, or any leader in a chosen profession at the top of his or her game is more knowledgeable about every aspect of the process needed to succeed. So pay your dues to learn your chosen field.

W29 Networking (Because You Never Know)

When you are making contact with people to get something accomplished (whether it's a deal you're eager to land or a contractor you want to handle a project for you), don't leave any stone unturned. You never know who might have the winning connection: an officer of a company, a friend, or a golfing buddy. Everyone has acquaintances. That's why it pays to treat everyone with respect.

W30　Learn from Your Mistakes

Refrain from doing the same thing, using the same rhythm, without recognizing that at some point along the way, your fortunes are likely to begin reversing. Realize how you can change or adapt to accomplish your goals. And remember that not everyone is on your wavelength, especially when they're on the other end of a situation. Instead of fighting those brick walls, bend a little. You will find that you will go even further than you anticipated. Successful people often say, "Every mistake is a step forward."

W31 Rank Has Its Privilege

In the military, in corporate life, or anywhere with an organizational structure, rank has its privileges. Any argument I've seen that got out of hand was won by the person in the higher position. Don't win the battle but lose the war. If you win the battle and the higher-ranking person is embarrassed or doesn't accept it, he or she will simply wait and burn you later. And that's a fact, Jack!

W32   There's No *I* in *Team*

If you're on a team at work, in sports, or at church, or other religious organization, taking an individual approach takes away from the full effect of the team concept. It often is more important to blend in as an integral part of the team. That's what teamwork is all about. Disregard the smart aleck's comebacks like "Yes, but there is an *i* in the word 'win'" or "*Team* does have an *m* and an *e*."

W33 Hit the Deck Running

When the General Quarters alarm is sounded on a naval ship, the crew members drop what they're doing and take their battle stations. Use this expression when you must motivate colleagues to focus on starting a chore quickly.

W34 There's More Than One Way to Skin a Cat

It's pretty gruesome, but in the 1800s, when cat fur was used in women's clothing, the concern was if the cat were still alive in during the processes. This s a reminder that there may be other approaches to take in order to reach the same desired objective.

W35 Keep It Simple Stupid

Also known as the KISS principle, this saying comes off kind of harsh, but all it means is not to dwell on every possible solution of a game plan. Pick the best one of your top choices and run with it instead of getting bogged down, wasting time.

W36 Don't Burn Your Bridges

This is a warning that means to me – don't hurt people along your way up because you may meet the same people on your way down.

W37 Don't Put the Cart before the Horse

As a unit – the horse pulls the cart. If you put the horse behind the cart the unit will not go far at all. Think of doing things in the proper order. Do not to be impatient.

PEOPLE

PI   The Caregiver Needs Help Too

The family member who takes care of an ill person goes through stress as well – and often, it's greater than that experienced by the indisposed person. Keep an eye on, and come to the aid of, the caregiver as well as the care receiver

P2 *Look* People

You've met them. When things get a bit hot and heavy, they stop and exclaim, "Look, it's going to be this way!" Although it's not easy to deal with "look people," they are easy to read. Trust that they mean what they say. If they are in a position of power and come up with a "Look, it's going to be this way" approach, back off and decide whether you want to take it or leave it. As far as they are concerned, the conversation is over. Now you have a decision to make.

P3 We All Wear Masks

We all wear masks, depending on the particular situation. An actor wears the mask of the character being portrayed. A teacher dons the educator's mask. When you're commiserating with friends, you put on your camaraderie mask. Keeping this in mind, if you face a problem, is it wiser to slip on an aggravated person's mask or that of a person politely seeking help? The latter mask gets more sympathy and gains you more acceptability, especially from those who listen to complaints all day.

P4 People Possess Pathologies

When facing a situation that you have been in before, you probably will do what you did the last time. You merely must decide if that is good or bad. When you get involved with a new boyfriend or girlfriend, your friends and family may show concern that the two of you are not a "good fit." If your answer to that is, "Oh, they will change," don't bet on it. People have their own pathologies (their own habits) and they might alter them temporarily to impress you, but in the long term change is very hard to effect. It's just in their nature.

P5 But You Never Told Them *No*

If you're being harassed, say "no" or "stop" to the person responsible and assert that you will tell someone in authority the next time the harassment occurs. I have had friends in sexual harassment situations whose silence was interpreted as consent because they never told the perpetrators "no." The offenders, in fact, used the target's failure to say "no" as an excuse when giving their side of the story, contending they had no idea the target was ever upset.

P6   In Life, People Are Givers or Takers

If you are a giver and hang around with a taker, be aware that your ideas will be tempered by the taker. Takers need to be the stars. Basically, they don't have time for anyone but themselves. It's OK to hang around with one, as long as you are getting what you want from the situation. Conversely, if you're a taker, remember that a giver rounds out your ideas and, usually, is very helpful bringing in perspective to your one-sided thinking. Which are you?

P7 People Can't Keep Secrets

Either the secret is too hot and must be revealed or it's deemed okay to tell to someone not connected to you. It's simply amazing how a secret makes the rounds to someone we know. And sometimes, people just forget they were told something in confidence and they'll relate it unaware they're breaking your trust. Be very careful with whom you trust with those close-to-your-heart secrets. This includes business situations.

P8 Pride Goeth before the Fall

Pride is a wonderful feeling, but be careful not to mix it with arrogance. It seems a routine condition that just before a wheeler/dealer takes a financial fall there is an attitude of arrogance that clouds the mind. An athlete who feels he is too good to practice or a student who feels no need to study for an exam is risking doing well.

P9   Horizontal versus Vertical Thinkers

Learn to recognize the difference between horizontal and vertical thinkers. Horizontal thinkers favor the level they are on. Vertical thinkers see a grander scale. So, if a person works in a mailroom and worries only about the mailroom, he or she is a horizontal thinker. A vertical thinker, knowing how the mailroom interacts with all other departments, recognizes the potential for obtaining a promotion. Pay attention to the category you normally fall into. Horizontal thinkers are *comfortable*. Vertical thinkers are *opportunity seekers*.

P10   Recognize Loser Conversation

Along life's journey, you will meet people who are constantly negative. They repeatedly say, "I can't accomplish the task because of this or that." They see every glass as half empty. And these people just don't get things done. They seek an excuse to cover their trail. They deliver all these premature reasons that project stinks or is overwhelming. Be wary of those conversations. Be mindful of what you say to them because they will almost certainly repeat any feedback you give them. It might even appear as if you're the one instigating the conversation. Likes attract likes. Concentrate on what you can do, not on what you can't. Offer them help or advice once, and drop it if they don't accept it.

♙II Blood Is Thicker Than Water

Family ties, or nepotism, can be found in every business situation, walk of life, or social environment. If you're partnered with a klutz with those ties who is flailing at work, trust me, you will get your share of the blame because of it. Be careful. If that klutz is connected, the family will protect the klutz to one degree or another. Of course, it's unfair. But life is often unfair. It is important for that person to realize that he depends on you so he can compliment you and recommend you to others.

P12 A Bully Is Very Insecure

Every time I encountered a bully and got tired of being pushed around, I challenged the bully. And every time he didn't know what to do! It's so unusual that the victim stands up for himself and fights back. In my younger years this situation was more physical. As I grew older, the situations grew emotional. The boss bully is so used to people kowtowing to him that he usually backs down and, in fact, often praises the victim. If anyone tries to bring you down, remember that you are better than that.

P13　The Advantage of Wealth

Wealthy people have the money to take risks and take time off to follow their dreams. They have enough financial backing that if a project fails, it won't bankrupt them. Others, especially the poor, don't enjoy that convenience. Don't waste time being jealous of wealthy people. If becoming wealthy is critically important to you, sit down and look at the route you must take to get there (legally, of course). Spend the time to build a war chest for investments or projects. For example, if you're interested in acquiring real estate, start with a two-flat, buy it, rehab it, and than sell it. Turn that money over into a four-flat, buy it, rehab it, and than sell it, and so on. I know a few people who have done just that and now, they just visit their buildings to make sure everything's operating properly. It's a nice life and it gives them the time to get involved with other projects. Remember all investments involve some level of risk.

P14   Learn to Recognize Insecure People

Generally, insecure people are untrustworthy, because they seem to play by their own rules. They cover themselves up with the cloak of power. It can prove extremely hazardous if you recognize that your boss is one of these people. Unfortunately, if you have a falling out and it's very serious, that person is better able to cover up and to burn you than you are. There's no way around it. Get away from such company because you may be in an unfair, no-win situation.

P15 Maids, Butlers, and Chauffeurs

You might think these are the perks of becoming wealthy, yet maids, butlers, and chauffeurs are a necessity on certain levels. Tycoons have gotten where they are because, for the most part, they concentrated exclusively on their vocation every minute of the day. They learned that taking time to do dishes and keep house and the like took them away from working on their various projects. Out of necessity, they hire people to do the time-consuming tasks in their lives, so they are free to concentrate on their mission. It's more of a necessity to them.

P16 Money Talks

If you're involved with people in a deal or project, they should put money into the venture, just as you should. If some of the interested parties don't have the money to invest but they possess enough time or expertise to balance their contribution to the project. Tap one person to be the money person, another to be the administrative person, and a third to handle sales. It's critical to document the agreement among all parties.

P17 Most People Are Outwardly Packaged / Don't Judge a Book by Its Cover

Look inside the package to truly determine what a person represents. It's not simply what you see physically that matters. It takes some time doing various activities together to learn what truly makes someone tick. Don't assume you truly know a person because she dresses like your late Aunt Helen and is nice. If your friends or associates tell you that you're getting transferred to another department and will be working with a jerk of a new boss, don't prejudge the boss. Build your own history with that person. There's always another side to any story, and you just might agree with your new boss. Get to know people before you form your opinion of them.

P18   Still Waters Run Deep / Look before You Leap

Of Latin origin, these are powerful ideas. A quiet body of water can conceal power. Composure and style are defined by your self-assurance in your skills. Do not underestimate the quiet or cautious person. Moroccans like to say, "Take precautions with a silent lake."

P19 Everyone Plays the Game, But Nobody's Rules Are the Same

When you find you are with a person and must watch what you say and do all the time, consider staying away from that person. When you can't, face the person and let him or her know that you resent being talked down to. Ask how you can arbitrate this so you both can have some peace, since you probably are aggravating that person in return. If it is an overwhelming situation, say goodbye to one another. By the way, this is also my bottom-line opinion on dating.

P20   The Person with the Gold Makes the Rules

This saying goes back to early civilizations when leaders looked for professionals to handle their growing wealth of gold, but the professionals had to play by rules of the wealthy powers. If you are in a standoff situation at work, the owner or colleague with higher authority usually will prevail.

P21 Many People Want to Date Up and Marry Up

Keep that in mind when you meet someone new. If you're a laborer for a ready-mix company and the other person is a lawyer, that's a pretty wide gap. Though not impossible, it's a pretty wide chasm to overcome. Right after my divorce, I was invited to a party with marketing and advertising people and attractive models, and one particularly beautiful woman asked me what I did for a living. I told her I worked for a mechanical contractor. She replied, "You work *for* a mechanical contractor?" When I confirmed it, she said, "Nice meeting you," and exited stage left. My friend who invited me overheard this exchange and said the woman was a snob. I told him I thought it was okay because she was here to meet somebody who could do her some good or she was looking for a mansion or whatever. She realized I didn't possess any of that. I liked her because she was honest with me. She did not waste her time or my time.

P22 If Someone Will Do It For You, That Someone May Do It To You

Socially, if someone leaves somebody else to be with you, be aware that that person might leave you to be with somebody else. This can prove especially heartbreaking. It's the same with gossip. If someone gossips about someone else, he or she will gossip about you to others.

P23 "That's Who?" to "Who's That?"

At times during your life's journey, you will go from "that's who?" to "who's that?"

If you were active in a club or an organization and now you revisit it, you likely expect that people will be happy to see you. Don't be crushed if you don't receive the recognition you enjoyed before. It's a "What have you done for me lately?" situation. When you are active in the group and walk into a room, someone will say, "Oh, of course, that's who that is." When you're not active anymore, expect someone to say, "Well, who's that?"

P24 Position of Power

Whenever a problem emerges with someone, I've noticed that where we discussed it matters. What do I mean? When I brought up a problem while visiting the other person in their office, I couldn't put my finger on it, but it felt like he or she had some advantage on me. When I brought up the problem in my particular space, I didn't sense that feeling. I think that your space is a position of strength, so if you wish to discuss a problem you are having with someone, try to do it in your space not theirs.

P25 The Lady Doth Protest Too Much, Methinks

This is a William Shakespeare quote you can use when someone is explaining to the point of going overboard why they want someone to do something. They may be hiding ulterior motives that are not being shared with the other person.

TIDBITS

TI Obvious

While *obvious* is not a good word for a criminal lawyer to use, it's perfect for a patent attorney. Be very careful when using this word. What is obvious to you may not be obvious to another. Make sure that you and the other person involved have the same understanding. Having documentation may help to understand the terms of any agreement.

T2   Your Dreams Are *Your* Dreams

You can't count on anyone else to get something done for you. You have to lighten up when you hear, "Quit dreaming and forget that project." If you've always had a goal and it remains your dream, regardless of how unlikely it is, then persevere. Always leave a little time to go forward with that vision. I am known as the dreamer in my family. I wouldn't have it any other way. I like to play with different ventures and I haven't 'hit' on one yet, but I am going to persist with my dreams. This book is among them. Writing it gives me great pleasure. These ambitions require a lot of time -- and often a lot of money. Be prepared if you're a dreamer. If one person benefits from this book I will be a happy man.

T3 Setting Up a Partnership

Always try to line up an odd number of partners. Then, any dispute will be resolved by majority vote and you won't sustain a stalemate. If you decide you don't want a third partner, then put it in writing that you both agree on a certain person to be the arbitrator if there is a dispute. If you two don't see eye to eye on something, then take the issue to the arbitrator to decide. You both must agree to abide by that decision.

T4 Practice

If you love what you do, honing your skills by practicing becomes a joy. You should look forward to it, whether it's a hobby, sport, or musical instrument. Practice leads you to excel and that can bring you joy.

T5 Help for Taking Tests

If you are taking a test with many questions and a time limit, look over the entire test and get the easy questions out of the way pronto. If you must spend extra time on the harder questions, spend that time at the end. You'll leave fewer unanswered questions.

T6 Learn the Tools of Your Trade or Sport

Master what's required of you in terms of power (brain and muscular), speed, and agility. Work on your weaknesses to enhance overall productivity. The late, great Chicago Bears football player, running back Walter Payton wasn't the fastest runner. But his discipline of speed and agility and all the preparation he put into it, including becoming an excellent blocker, made him exceptional. Chicago Bulls basketball player Michael Jordan excelled at all the offensive and defensive skills. If his shooting skills were a bit off, he merely would pass the ball to a teammate who had a clear shot at the basket. That honed his playmaking skills.

T7 The Mirror

Look in the mirror and try to see the complete - not just the physical - person. Are you, in fact, that person you want to be in the eyes of others? You must be true to that person in the mirror, and be comfortable as that person. That is the most important person in your life. If you are at peace with the image, it is much easier to get along with other people. Build a solid personal foundation.

T8 Try Being Subtle

Being indirect is a wonderful skill to master. Not possessing that skill ranks among my shortcomings. So be better than me. Once you decide you need or want to say something, ask yourself how you can phrase it in the most diplomatic and constructive way possible. Learning to take that time will improve your communication immensely.

T9 Engage with Nature

Nature is what it is. It takes its own time. Sometimes it's brutal. Sometimes it's calm. It never lies. We have to get along with it. It doesn't have to get along with us. Unlike people, who possess ulterior motives for their interest in you, nature says, "You will blend in with me." That's why I recommend getting out in nature, to regroup and meditate. Many people like to meditate near water, in the woods, or in a meadow. Listening to meditation recording, of which there are many, may be helpful.

T10   Test Your Memory

If you have trouble remembering a person's name, start with A and go through the alphabet. If it's a man, go over all the men's names you can recall that begin with A, and then go to B and C and down the line. Hopefully his name will click in. The same thing goes for a woman's name. It really works. I find this system works with places, names of movie stars, or just about anything. Give it a try.

TII God, Grant Me the Serenity to Accept the Things I Cannot Change, the Courage to Change the Things I Can and the Wisdom to Know the Difference

You will face situations in which you will emerge the loser, and you may be bullheaded and still attempt to get your own way. If it's an overwhelming situation you cannot change, try to either go along with it or possess the courage to hang in there if you believe change is possible. Hopefully this prayer can teach you to treat a catastrophe as you would treat an annoyance.

T12 About Grief

When you lose a loved one, you almost certainly will go through phases: denial, anger, depression, and then slow acceptance of what has happened. Getting through to that acceptance phase and getting on with your life, has to be in your own time. Yes, there are some wonderful books on grief. They can help you understand the stages of grief. Don't feel that you have to rush grief, but also recognize when you are wallowing. And when a friend or relative experiences a loss, just being there for them is the very best approach. God forbid you will ever say to someone, "Would you snap out of it and get on with your life?"

T13   Grief after a Breakup

A breakup of a relationship or a marriage is sad for both sides. But it's a lot easier for the one saying good-bye than for the one being told good-bye. The sorrow stretches on longer for the one who has had good-bye said to him or her. There is *hell* in *hello* and *good* in *good-bye,* so be careful with *hello* and don't be afraid of *good-bye;* find the goodness in it.

T14   Kitchen Oven Fire

If a fire erupts in your oven, simply close the oven door and turn off the oven. The lack of oxygen will make the fire go out. Also don't throw water on a grease fire (when the water hits the grease, it will flare up) or try to remove the burning pan to put it into the sink (you may drop it or dump the whole thing). Kitchen lessons teach life lessons as well.

T15 Do Not Swear

Someone who refrains from profanity stands out as a very strong person. Self-restraint enhances your inner strength, your composure, and your appearance to other people. You may think, *"That advice sounds good, but in the environment I live in, it's just very hard to do."* To that, I say, it's even more important that you show true character.

T16   Drink Plenty of Water

I've read that we should drink eight, eight-ounce glasses of water a day. Boy that's a lot! I have a six ounce glass of water at ten am and three pm. Water helps our organs function properly. And if you've been drinking alcoholic beverages, sip a big glass of water at bedtime because alcohol causes dehydration. Although you may have to visit the bathroom during the night, that glass of water will help the way you feel the next morning. Drinking water certainly helps you to stay as hydrated as you can while playing sports.

T17   Use Shoe Trees

You'll be pleased to see how much longer your shoes will stay attractive if you fit shoetrees in them when you are not wearing them.

T18   Sugarless Gum

Get into the habit of chewing a piece of sugarless gum for about fifteen minutes after every meal. The gum will keep your saliva flowing and, thereby, keep a cleaning action going in your mouth. You should notice brighter teeth and fresher breath.

T19   Three Basics of Dining

Rule 1: When you sit down at the table, pick up the napkin and put it on your lap. You can still do this while talking.

Rule 2: If you leave the table to return, put that same napkin on your chair, not anywhere on the table because it might touch something that can stain and transfer that stain to your clothes.

Rule 3: Never leave the soupspoon in the bowl if there is a plate underneath the bowl. Put in on the plate. If there is no plate underneath the bowl it is acceptable to leave the spoon in the bowl.

T20   About Remodeling

For any estimate you receive to remodel a kitchen, a bedroom, a house, or whatever it is, simply double it (that's right – double it). This isn't to say you're naive or the contractor you hire is a crook. It means at the start of a project you can't know the unforeseeable conditions that can erupt. When you break into an existing wall, for instance, you might find termite, moisture, or mold damage that must be repaired before you start with the new work. Ask the contractor to discuss possible surprises with you and not to proceed with a change without your approval.

T21 About Gambling

Gamble with your brain, not your emotions. It's no surprise that the gaming industry uses strategies to get your mind off what you're doing: free drinks, beautiful people walking around, spectacular shows, beautiful architecture, and conversation. Indeed, anything that will break your concentration will be tried. It's very difficult to resist that environment. Most gamblers are excitable people who bet with their heart and emotions at the same time. So, a good motto is: Leave the gambling to the professionals. And of course never ever bet more than you can afford to lose.

T22 Keep Exercise in Your Routine

Stretching your body is important. You may feel infallible now, but you won't necessarily be as you age. I am fortunate that I have stayed at the same weight since military boot camp. But I work at it, exercising, playing racquetball, biking, playing tennis, rowing and jogging. The secret is to keep it in your routine - no matter how tired you are, get out and do it. Do cardiovascular exercises even if you work construction jobs. The older you get, the more important it is to keep exercise in your routine. You can simply adjust your routine. As I aged I switched from jogging to biking. It was much easier on my legs and I saw a lot more of my hometown of Chicago and the lakefront parks because I covered more ground.

T23 Weigh Buying an Expensive Item

The issue is with the difference in price. I've passed up numerous special items because I thought, *"I'm not going to pay that much for that!"* Later I regretted the decision because the item was special enough to me that I should have paid the higher price to possess it. I soon realized it was what I perceived to be an inflated price that I objected to paying, and at that time the amount had simply outweighed my interest in the item itself. So consider what you think the item should be worth and compare that price with the listed price. If you want the item badly enough, pay the difference. If not, walk away.

T24 There Is Only One Way to Swing a Tennis Racquet

A tennis pro said to me, "I have advice for your book. There are many ways to swing a tennis racquet but only one way to swing it correctly. So tell your readers to stick to learning something the right way and don't improvise. The right way will take you a lot further." That goes for all sports ... and much of life, too.

T25 The Stock Market

I do pretty well as an individual investor who just reads magazines and watches the television business shows. Years ago, the brokers watched these shows and now we can, too, thanks to the Internet. The only thing I try to do is let the numbers tell me what to do. Each stock goes up and down and now you get into a timing situation because you want to buy on the dips. You know, the old "buy low, sell high" maxim. Hopefully, those highs and lows will be going in an upward direction more times than not. It's like those little white birds that ride on a rhinoceros's back and peck the insects out of its eyes and ears to keep the rhino clean. They don't try to dictate the direction the rhino goes. That's the way I flow with the market. I let it do what it wants to do. I try to make decisions based on what the market's doing. I try to recognize trends in various categories/companies with less competition in their field. You are playing with fire if you get involved with penny stocks because of the risk and a bad track record. The best advice I can give is to invest with a professional advisor.

T26 Button That Sport Coat, Guys

A suit, sport coat, or tuxedo is designed to have the jacket buttoned. The only times you should unbutton it is to put a topcoat over it, sitting down, or taking it off. When you are standing, the jacket should be buttoned. Designers and tailors make a lot of money to give you that elegant look. Use it. And look around you at the next function you attend. You will see that the dapper men keep their jackets buttoned. If you want to be an average guy bellying up to the bar, don't button it.

T27 It's Okay for a Boy to Cry

Anyone who tells a young boy to "stop that, don't cry, girls cry" is under the mistaken impression it will help the boy stop crying. They don't realize that it puts doubt in the young boy's mind that he may not be normal or that there's something wrong with him. It is perfectly okay to cry – whoever you are and whatever your age.

T28   Talk to Children As If They're Young Adults

Communicate with children without using patronizing phrases or baby talk. They will grow and mature faster and also love you for it.

T29 Clothes

Buy quality apparel that will last long and will stay in style. There are many discount retailers and outlet stores today selling temporary current fashion. But look at the difference in the quality of the stitching, the cut, how the garment is put together, and the caliber of materials. I own shirts that have lasted a long time because my size generally stays constant and I buy good quality. It is the dirt in the garment that breaks down its consistency, so cleaning is important. A good-quality garment will last you a long time.

T30   Get Your Rest

You will look younger and healthier. When you get older, you readily recognize the effects of habits of poor eating and, perhaps, drinking alcohol excessively. People who don't get their rest suffer a lot of physical problems. But rest and exercise with the proper diet can extend your wellbeing ... and your life.

T31 Keep Reading

Put reading material into your routine. Make a habit of learning a new word a day – no matter your age. It will help you make an important point more precisely. When you don't know the meaning of a word, don't hesitate to ask for clarification. In fact, asking for clarification lets the person know you're listening.

T32 Walk and Talk with Your Lord

I enjoy asking Jesus to walk with me a while or to be present at a meeting I'm attending. With God's presence there, it's amazing how my behavior is positively influenced. Prayer is good.

T33   The Paper Doesn't Refuse the Ink

This is a good saying to use when a friend can't make up his or her mind. You are reminding the person that all the facts are in, so decide already.

T34   I'm Just Touching Base with You

In baseball, when a player is on first base, the first baseman is always alert to keep the base runner from stealing second base. The first baseman must keep an eye on the pitcher in case the pitcher tries to pick the runner off of first base. Let's say the pitcher throws the next pitch past the batter and the catcher returns the ball to the pitcher. While that transpires, the runner returns safely and stands on first base to get ready for the next pitch. This is when the first baseman can relax until the next pitch. So the movement of the runner isn't threatening to the first baseman, as if to communicate, "I'm just touching base." What this means to me is that I am starting the conversation with you with no malice intended, just saying hello to see that everything is okay.

T35   How Do You Like Them Apples?

In the motion picture *Good Will Hunting*, Matt Damon's character wins a verbal confrontation with a college student over a girl. Afterward Matt rubs it in by asking the student if he likes apples. The student reluctantly nods and Matt Damon shows the student the phone number of a that girl they were both flirting with and loudly proclaims, "I got her number. How do you like them apples?" I don't know how this saying got started, but it seems to be very poignant when you want to tease someone after a victory.

In Conclusion

This knowledge, I believe, will help enhance your ability to articulate your thoughts.

So go get 'em.' And in case no one has said this to you yet today, God bless you.

If you would like to share any of your sayings from your real world and would like me to share them with other readers, please write to:

Len Tomaka, 175 E. Delaware Place, Chicago IL 60611

Thanks,
Len

About the Author

Len Tomaka has reached retirement age after an active life. He grew up on Chicago's south side, where he learned to be street savvy. His college was a Chicago Local Union #597 pipe fitter apprenticeship. He grabbed fourth place in the city YMCA weightlifting competition, spent five years in the United States Marine Corps Reserve, and owned a cosmetics franchise. He was a pipe fitter, an estimator /  project manager for mechanical contractors, and the owner of his own consultancy (Tomaka Associates) to mechanical contractors. Also, he holds three US patents. Len doesn't consider himself a teacher, a raconteur, or a psychologist. But he does have common sense.